Michael: Who Would You Leave Behind?

The Story of One Family's Fight Against Drug Abuse

By Brad Alumbaugh and Debbie Alumbaugh

Copyright 2007
by Brad Alumbaugh and Debbie Alumbaugh
Michael's Message
www.**michaelsmessage**.org

ISBN 978-1-930572-47-6
Library of Congress Control No. 2006933145

Printing (Last Digit)
9 8 7 6 5 4 3 2 1

The authors reserve all rights to the materials in this book under U.S. copyright laws. In an effort to provide educational material which are as practical and economical as possible, we grant to *individual* purchasers of this book the right to make copies of materials contained therein for their personal use only. Copying this book or its parts for resale is strictly prohibited.

Published by—
Educational Media Corporation®
PO Box 213111
Minneapolis, MN 55421-0311
(763) 781-0088 or (800) 966-3382
www.**educationalmedia**.com

Production editor—
Don L. Sorenson, Ph.D.
Graphic design—
Earl Sorenson
Cover Photograph—
Matthew Field
www.**photography.mattfield**.com

Acknowledgments

Our Deepest appreciation to...

Our youth, our future, for asking for more. Without their honesty and compassion the book would not have been possible.

Col. James McDonough for your unwavering commitment to keeping our youth safe and drug-free. Your help in getting this message out to our youth is invaluable. Your dedication, expertise, and friendship to us are most appreciated and very highly valued. We are honored to have met you.

Erica Orloff for your infinite enthusiasm and never ending support in completing this work. Your "nothing is impossible" attitude will always be admired. Your excellent work ethic and positive attitude have helped us get through the challenges of writing and rewriting. You are a most trusted friend who takes the words loyalty and dedication to a new level.

Earl Sorenson whose assistance with the publishing business we could not do without. We value your friendship, support, and integrity more than you will ever know.

Our Daughter and Son-In-Law, Eliese and David, who have loved, honored, and supported us through the loss of our son and the rest of this journey. You exemplify the word "Love."

Table of Contents

Chapter One
Michael: Leaving Us Behind 11

Chapter Two
Imagine 23

Chapter Three
The Circle Of Life 29

Chapter Four
A Victory 37

Chapter Five
Lonely Holidays 41

Chapter Six
Communication From Beyond 45

Chapter Seven
Peer Pressure 53
   Telling Mom and Dad: Drugs At School 54
   Strategies 56
   School Policy and Parent Role 56
   Teachers Need Help! 57

Chapter Eight
Michael's Dream 59

Chapter Nine
Living The Dream 65
    Surviving Our Third Christmas Without Michael . 66
    A Sign Of Healing 66

Chapter Ten
Mary, the Cocaine Addict 69

Chapter Eleven
The Little College Student and Waitress 73

Chapter Twelve
Her Twin Sister 77

Chapter Thirteen
Graduation 2001 81
    Father's Day: The Yearbook 83

Chapter Fourteen
Our Schools 85
    Heroin In The Boy's Bathroom 88

Chapter Fifteen
Looking Back on Michael's Last Day 91
    Knowing Michael Was a Privilege 92

Chapter Sixteen
The Ending 95

Introduction

My wife and I hope and pray by writing this book and sharing the heartbreak of losing a child to drugs that we all can learn from this tragedy. By sharing Michael's last day, students will realize how quickly a wrong choice can and will change families and friends lives forever. Our students need new tools to keep them focused in their lives. Education will help refocus our youth and help them reach their highest potential. Parents also need a new awareness of the existing problem our youth are faced with each day. Baby boomer parents, the most drug-savvy generation yet, are confronting an entirely new universe of drugs as their children explore GHB, Ecstasy, and Ketamine, in addition to marijuana, cocaine, heroin and LSD. This tragedy happened because of wrong choices.

We will explain in great detail Michael's last day, the red flags that were ignored, laughed at, and the courage that none of his friends had. Our school campuses are overloaded with promises of the "best" high you can imagine. But what happens when that high leads to death? What about the precious and promising lives that are cut short?

We start our journey by asking "WHY?" You will be amazed at how and where the answers come from.

We will open Michael's bedroom door and relive that dreadful morning finding him. The pain we endure from our immense loss. How the holidays turn our stomachs, no longer giving us happiness. Experiencing birthdays, his prom, and the one-day we strived most for—his graduation. We lost those memories.

As parents who have experienced the unexpected loss of a child we have journeyed down a path of love and spirituality. Learning to look inward and finding forgiveness. We will tell of the dream that changed our lives our "spiritual awakening." By reading this book, you will ascertain that we truly don't die and there is no more. Our body dies, but our spirit lives on. Michael is proof. Michael has communicated with us time and again since making his transition.

The Story of One Family's Fight Against Drug Abuse

We have learned that peer pressure is intense and the fear of not fitting in is stealing our future. This problem not only affects our young ones, but in college it gets much worse. Drug use is a growing problem with our youth. Ours is not an isolated case, you will hear other stories from students and parents about this evil that faces us all. Education is the key to prevention.

We have shared our message with over 35,000 students across Florida in our first year. We have had the honor of testifying before Congress and being on CNN. We have been featured in many newspapers including the Associated Press. We have been the topic of TV shows from Jacksonville to West Palm Beach, Florida.

We hope you will join us as we explore our spiritual growth. How we are taking an unbearable tragedy and with the help of our spirit guides, devotion and love turning this into a positive learning experience for all of us.

We would like to share a letter with you that we received from James R. McDonough, Director of Florida Drug Control:

> *This is a heart-wrenching story to read, for it reveals the grief of a loving mother and father in their lonely vigil to find meaning in their son's death to drug abuse. But it is also a timely story, for we live in an age when youth in America are at risk to manipulation by those who would have them believe that their popularity, happiness, and worth can come only with mind-altering experiences that will, sooner or later, place them in harm's way.*
>
> *Brad and Debbie Alumbaugh are ordinary people who suffered an extraordinary loss but go on to display a remarkable courage in sharing their story so that others might be spared a similar fate. There is no misdirection in what they say, no attempt to proselytize, nor even to condemn. They merely relate what they have gone through, what they didn't know before it was too late, and what they have learned since. You are there with them in the final day of their son's life, at the scene of his death, and in the journey they lead from that moment on, each step a groping to*

come to terms with reality, and finally an undertaking and a commitment to warn others of the dangers they—and Michael—did not see coming.

For generations, America's youth did not see and did not want to accept the grave consequences of smoking. Our culture glamorized it; the industry seduced with that same glamour. To smoke was to be adult, to be chic, to be special. Only when the death rate topped 400,000 a year and the extent of the exploitation by mercenary profiteers were exposed did youth rebel and began to quit smoking in droves, now at less than half the rate of only a decade ago.

But youth alcohol use and drug use continue unabated, presented as cigarettes once were, as a means to 'coolness', social acceptability, and maturity. Indeed, experts on the development of the adolescent brains, such as Dr. Aaron White of Duke University, have pointed out that a growing youthful infatuation with prescription as "recreational enhancement" (as opposed to "use as prescribed") puts US on the cusp of a deadly surge in damage and death to America's youth. The experts warn, but youth in its rash belief of its own immortality moves on to assert its misconception of liberated independence, never realizing the extent of its own victimization.

This book gave the lie to all that. It is not a presentation of statistics, of moral uprightness, or frightening harangue. No, it is merely a cautionary tale by two decent people who loved their son and who find, I would hope, solace in telling his—and their—story. And by so doing they express their decency toward and concern for all children and the parents who would grieve by their loss.

James R. McDonough
Director of Florida Drug Control

Preface

Who would you leave behind?

Think about that question. If you died tomorrow, who would you leave behind?

We wrote this book for teenagers everywhere, and if you've picked up this book, we hope it's because you want to learn more about our son's story, our family's story, and the fight against drugs that's being waged every day in your middle school or high school, at every party whose invitation you may or may not accept, on the street corner, in your own home.

It is easy to think of the "war on drugs" as something politicians talk about. The President of the United States talks about the war on drugs. But what does that have to do with you—or us? Or our son Michael?

As you read on, we don't think you'll be able to put this book down. You're going to see yourself in these pages, as well as see your friends, your school, and your family. You're going to see yourself in these pages because, sadly, we don't think there is a teenager, and maybe even pre-teenager, in all of America, who isn't familiar with drugs. Even if you choose not to try drugs, you see them around you. You hear about how cool it is to try them in songs or in movies. You may see them around you so much that they become commonplace. And that's dangerous. Because when drugs become commonplace, you or your friends might be tempted.

Our son Michael died from a drug overdose. He was a black belt in karate, an honors student, and most importantly, he was our son. You see, in the end it doesn't matter whether you earn straight A's or what hobbies you have or how many baseballs you can hit out of the park or ballet recitals you star in. In the end, we are all measured by how much we are loved by those around us. Michael was loved very much. Each of you reading this is, too.

Who would you leave behind if you died accidentally from an overdose? Mother, father, brothers and sisters, grandparents who adore you, friends, girlfriends, boyfriends, teachers who believe in you. The list goes on and on. Even if sometimes, as a teen, you feel alienated from the adults around you, trust us, the love is still there. You see each of us is like a thread, woven into the fabric of our lives, joining with the threads of everyone who loves us.

This book isn't about scaring you. It's about the truth. You may feel sad when you read it, and that's OK. You may feel angry that drugs are so readily available. No matter what, though, we are sure you will have a lot to think about. Our mission is to make you think. Our mission is to make sure that no other family in America faces what we have. We go on because we must, and we deliver... Michael's message.

Chapter One

Michael: Leaving Us Behind

What is the essence of being a teenager? I am sure a lot of your parents will say, with love and maybe a little weary affection, it's about you eating them out of house and home, asking to borrow the car keys, asking for money so you can go to the movies or buy a new CD, sports, getting your first boyfriend or girlfriend, asking for those car keys again, going to the prom (and asking us for more money—and those car keys again!), and very messy rooms. It's also about being loved by your family despite teens' raging hormones and the occasional door slamming or argument. We know adolescence is hard. But we parents love you kids anyway.

And what about you teens reading this book? What would you say is the essence of being a teenager? Probably something about trying to keep up in school, hating homework, falling in love for the first time, learning how to drive, going to the prom, bugging your parents for a car, getting your first part-time job, secret crushes, parties, and your friends, your friends, your friends.

All those things are probably part of it. But each of you is as unique as your fingerprint, just as our Michael was. We can't possibly tell you everything about him—that would take two books, or a whole library! —And it's hard to describe a person anyway, who he or she really is inside. But here are a few pieces of the story of our son.

For one thing, he was born premature, but later grew up to earn a black belt in karate. He was a pretty determined guy, and his room was almost a trophy case of medals and awards for his favorite sport. He even went on to teach classes in karate. He believed in the discipline, and it was a passion of his.

He loved to shoot hoops. He loved his friends—and when he was with them, he always made it a point to entertain them with jokes and silliness.

He was an honors student. He was also very compassionate. One girl shared with us how, instead of shunning her when she was pregnant like many in the school, Michael asked about her baby daily and talked to her, wanting to know how she was doing, and making her feel special. Our next-door neighbor, a senior citizen, told how he would show her his karate moves and visit her for hours. Seniors are often lonely, but he made sure this woman knew he cared. He made her laugh, and he entertained her.

He was close with us. We married when Michael was nine; his mom, Debbie, had gotten a divorce from Michael's biological father when she was still pregnant with Michael. Soon after our wedding, he took to calling me "Dad." It was as if, we think, God intended for us to be a family all along. Brad and Michael just fit together as if each of their hearts was missing a piece, like a puzzle, and when they found each other and we became a family the puzzle was complete.

Michael also touched the lives of his cousins and friends and aunts and uncles. He was loved and cherished. He was like all of you reading this. He was a teen. A real person. And his death cut off a life so full of promise.

Adults often say that teens think they are *invincible*. That means teens think they can't die. They don't consciously think that, but most teens feel "that could never happen to me." Teens are such terrific people, on their way to becoming adults and growing and learning, but they're so full of the energy of life, they may drive too fast or not wear a seatbelt—they may take all kinds of chances. They may do careless things because of this feeling of invincibility. They may even try drugs.

We found out from Michael's friends that they had tried smoking pot, or marijuana. Many teens, and sadly, some adults, think marijuana isn't dangerous because they say it's not addictive. Michael and his friends also believed this, but they had a pact: They would try pot, but they would never do any other drugs. We know how tempting it is for teens to protect each other, to make secret promises like these. But sometimes that feeling of invincibility can hide the hidden dangers of this drug and others. And secret pacts don't help.

Because Michael had tried pot, it may have made it seem like less of a "big deal" when someone offered him pills, methadone, for a headache he had. His head just throbbed and ached, and he wanted to be rid of it. Rather than going to the school nurse, he took pills that were offered to him. *He made a wrong choice.*

Do you ever wish you could turn back the clock? We do every day. We wish we were there to stop Michael, to warn him that he didn't know what he was taking. This was the first time—the very first time—he had ever experimented with pills. Your parents, your grandparents, adults everywhere often wish we could be with you all the time to make sure you always make smart decisions. But part of growing up is allowing you to make some decisions on your own. That's part of eventually being an adult. We can't always be there, much as we ache now and wish we had been. But that's impossible. What Michael—and maybe you—didn't know is that a single incident of experimenting with drugs can be fatal. Look around you. Who would you leave behind? Think of how excruciating it would be for any parent to want to turn back the clock. Who wouldn't want just one more hug? One more I love you. One more smile. And the chance to ask a simple question: *Why?*

As Michael took the methadone for his headache, he got a high. He took a few more during the course of the day. Methadone, like many drugs, tends to increase feelings of invincibility. Most drugs also lower your inhibitions, or that part of you that tells you to be careful. Methadone also leaves the user with a sense of well-being.

Michael's friends saw that he was passing out at times during that last day; they saw many things. But teens tend to keep a wall of silence around their activities. Friends are often, to teens, the most important people in their lives. It's part of adolescence. It's not that teens don't love their parents anymore and vice versa, but that clique, group of pals or teammates, or best friend often take on even more importance. They may honor their pact or promise to keep quiet about friends using drugs so as not to betray a promise to a friend, or to not seem "uncool," or maybe just because they're not used to confiding in adults.

Adolescence is a rocky time. How many teens are going to tell their parents that one of their friends is trying drugs and doesn't seem well? Though we asked his friends whether Michael was on some kind of drugs because he didn't seem well, they all looked us in the eye and said no, obeying an unspoken "Code of Silence." Now, they wish they, too, could go back in time and change things. They were left behind as well.

When we look back on this fateful day, we will never really know why Michael chose to take the drug GHB. We cannot and will not make an excuse for him. But it was, like taking those first few pills, the wrong choice and that added to his last day on earth. Of course, if you're reading this, it is easy to say, "That wasn't very good judgment." The important thing to remember, what we hope to show teens everywhere, is when you do drugs, even drugs you think of as harmless, like pot, your judgment is impaired. For instance, everyone knows that drinking and driving don't mix. Getting in a car with a drunk driver is something dangerous and downright stupid! But pour a couple of drinks into your system and that usual good judgment you show can disappear.

A fog of drugs clouded Michael's mind. He didn't intend to take drugs dangerously. But little by little, the drugs replaced his judgment, the judgment of an honors student, an athlete, and a loving young man. The drugs told him to go lie down. His friends didn't tell us they were worried (though we found out later he had passed out in front of them).

Who would you leave behind?

Michael was part of a tight-knit group of friends and cousins. And one of them, as well as his girlfriend, was with Michael that day. They were hanging out at our house and when it was time for them to go home, Brad walked them out to their car and asked, again, if Michael was on anything. At that moment, Brad's thoughts weren't anger at Michael. He was worried. He wanted to make sure Michael was safe, and if that meant taking him to a doctor, or staying with him all night long while he slept off the effects of these drugs, he would have done so. Their reply was "No Uncle Brad, honest, we just smoked some pot."

Brad walked back inside the house, turning off the lights outside. He stood at the edge of the bed contemplating whether to ask Debbie to get up out of bed, get a chair and sit by Michael's bed to make sure he would be all right. Brad decided that perhaps Michael just needed a good night's sleep to get the marijuana out of his system. After all, his friends had just reassured him that they had "only" smoked some pot. Brad decided that he and Michael would have a nice, long father-son chat in the morning. Brad wasn't afraid to talk to Michael about drugs. They were close. Brad didn't get that chance. Our son died that night. We were left behind.

Friday morning, the phone rang, waking Brad. He thought Michael would answer the phone, but instead the machine came on. As soon as it shut off, the phone rang again. This time Brad answered the phone, figuring it was one of Michael's friends. The voice on the other end said: "Michael's not at the bus stop." This was odd, but no cause for alarm yet. If only we could turn back time.

Walking toward Michael's room, rubbing his eyes, Brad was thinking they would have their talk later. First, it was time to get our son out of bed and off to school. The closer Brad got to Michael's door, the louder his alarm was blasting. Michael had full intentions of getting up and going to school that morning.

Here are Brad's thoughts and recollections of this terrible moment that changed the lives of everyone who knew Michael, and most especially his family, forever:

It is still hard for me to open this door. The agonizing thought of the way I found my son, still brings me out of a deep sleep. At times, Debbie wakes me because I scream out. When this happens, I have to get up, pace the floor, watch TV, read a book, and sometimes I'll take the dog for a walk, even at three in the morning.

Opening my son's door, finding this horrendous sight, made my heart feel like it was going to pound out of my chest. The blood rushing through my body made me think the top of my head was going to explode. I was literally scared that I was going to have a heart attack. My first instinct was to run out of the house and keep on running. My mind and body did not want to accept what my eyes had just found.

Through my sleepy eyes, I found Michael's eyes. My heart must have jumped to 200 beats per minute. Can you imagine finding your child? Your parents finding you?

His body lay lifeless on his waterbed. His eyes looked almost like he was daydreaming; only I knew that this was not the case. His mouth hanging open, his tongue swollen to such a point I couldn't close his mouth. My baby boy had a stream of dried vomit trailing down his chin, down the front side of his neck, a puddle of it next to his collarbone. As I looked closer at my son, I found his arms stretched out to each side of his body. My son's hands were in a clawed position where he had tried to roll over to save himself. But this is what this drug does to you. It paralyzes the motor system and robs you of the gag reflex. Michael couldn't save himself, nor could he even call out to his mother to help him.

> *I felt Michael's cold body, hoping to find a pulse. I pushed deep into his neck. I honestly knew he was dead, but I hoped that I would find just a trace of life. I looked back at his bedroom door, praying that his mother wasn't there. I paced back and forth at the foot of his bed saying, "No Michael, not you, not my son!" I felt that I was not alone; I could almost see spirits sitting on the top of my son's headboard with Michael at their side watching me.*

Just then, the doorbell rang! Brad ran to the front door as fast as he could, closing Michael's door behind him. Brad didn't want Michael's mother up yet. The idea that she would see her baby like this was too much to bear. Opening the front door, two of Michael's friends were there, including the friend who gave him GHB, and who was now standing at the end of our driveway next to the mailbox, red-faced, wringing his hands looking as though he was about to cry. Brad was led by an inner voice to tell them Michael was sick he wouldn't be going to school. With a pain like a knife in his heart, Brad realized Michael would never be going to school again.

Brad closed the door, his heart pounding wildly, hoping Michael's mother would not wake. As he hurried back to Michael's room, he prayed; "God, please give me my son back! I'll do anything... anything!" This is called "bargaining" with God. Imagine your parents saying to God that they would do anything to bring you back. It's hard to understand as a teen, but being a parent usually brings out an instinct to protect your child no matter what. They would have traded places with Michael in a moment. Brad searched deep in Michael's neck for a pulse, knowing in his own heart that there was none. Michael was gone.

Brad remembers feeling a presence in the room. He began to talk to Michael, and he kissed Michael's forehead. He stood there frozen in the moment, knowing that when he called for help, he would never be able to have this time alone with him again, ever! He also thought how marriages often couldn't withstand the death of a child. Everything in our lives was forever changed. No, Michael could never have meant to burden us with this pain that never goes away. But his usually wonderful judgment wasn't as sharp as it should have been because of drugs. Our enemy. Everything was moving in slow motion. Now an agonizing task lay in front of Brad—telling Michael's mother.

He knew he needed help. Brad ran to the garage, got in the car and drove to Michael's aunt and uncle's house. He wanted someone with him when he told Michael's mother. As they were leaving to hurry back before Debbie woke up, Michael's cousin met Brad in the hallway; he was as white as a sheet. If only someone had gathered the courage to tell Brad the night before when he asked, Michael would more than likely be alive and well today.

Entering Michael's bedroom, we can't imagine the thoughts rushing through his aunt and uncle's minds. Michael's uncle grabbed Michael's cold hand and held it; repeating over and over in a high-pitched voice with tears streaming down his face, "Oh no! Oh no!" His aunt was at the foot of the bed, her hand covering her mouth so as not to scream and go into a hysterical outburst. She was pacing almost as though she wanted to run from this horrible scene.

Michael's uncle is a paramedic and seemed to go into automatic mode doing what he had been trained to do. Brad watched Jay between his own tears, as Jay desperately tried to bring life back into Michael's body. Jay seemed so angry; he had saved so many lives, but he couldn't save his nephew who was only fifteen. Finally, out of pure exhaustion, Jay looked at Brad and expressed that it was time to tell Michael's mother. Brad's heart began to pound even faster, *how would he do this?* This took all the courage Brad had; he was at a loss for words. As he stood next to

Debbie, gently waking her, she could tell there was something drastically wrong. Brad said, "Jay and Susan are out in the living room, we need to talk."

Of course, Michael's mom knew something was wrong. Brad was so out of sorts, so filled with anxiety. Debbie asked, "Honey what is it? What is wrong with you?" Brad asked her to hurry. Downstairs, in the living room, the tension was making us all feel ill. Brad sat Debbie down on the couch and looked into her eyes. Brad paced back and forth, searching for the words. There were no words that would ease this blow. Nothing he could say could make this any easier. Finally, Brad and Jay blurted out, "It's Michael! He died in his sleep."

Of course, we were all now falling apart. Debbie screamed, then cried. Her mother instinct took over her emotions, so she wanted to go in his room to be near him to hold and comfort him, to clean him up. Brad told her the scene was something she shouldn't see. She should remember Michael, as he was, the boy with the beautiful innocent face. Debbie asked Brad if he looked scared. Brad couldn't tell her the truth: In his own words:

I lied. I told her he looked very peaceful. I could not tell her about the terrifying face with a swollen tongue and dried vomit on his face and neck. Jay and I convinced her not to go into his room. Jay called 911.

Imagine this horror in your own house. Imagine your parents. Maybe it feels uncomfortable to think about this. Who wants to think about this? But the mission of this book and our time spent speaking to students all over the country about the effects of drugs is that we *must* speak about this. We must speak about this until the horror in our own lives, in our own home, doesn't happen to another parent. We want every teen to know they are not invincible. You must be on your guard each and every time someone offers you a drink or drugs. If this could happen to Michael, it can happen to anyone. Look around your school. Look at your friends. Any one of you. And if that happened, who would you leave behind?

Chapter Two

Imagine

We'll tell you more about the terrible days and weeks following Michael's tragic death, but we wanted to touch base with you about drugs. We wanted to get you thinking in this chapter... and if you share this book with your parents, we want to get them thinking as well.

So many kids say, "Mom and Dad are so out of touch." "They just don't get it." Many parents chuckle about this. Because, believe it or not, we know a lot more about the ups and downs of adolescence than you think. We know what it's like to be "in love" with someone who doesn't even know you exist, to go to the prom, to wait by the phone, to study hard, to have a teacher you dislike... and one who inspires you, to get behind the wheel of a car for the first time, to want to sleep in until noon and stay up way too late. We even know—or think we know—about how drugs can be tempting to a group of kids.

Many of your parents grew up or were part of the 1960s. It was called the time of "counterculture," and part of that counterculture was rejecting the conservative 1950s and questioning *everything*. That pretty much sounds like any teenager, doesn't it? You question your parents, and you question the world. You're trying to figure out who you are and who you want to be.

In the 1960s and 1970s, people were familiar with pot or marijuana. Cocaine became "popular" in the "Disco era." (We know... disco is dead!). We ourselves would read about this in the newspaper or see reports on television about drugs, but if it didn't directly affect us, we probably ignored it. But as we journeyed through our grief—though we must tell you, we never, ever stop grieving—and set up Michael's Message, Inc. to educate people about the dangers of drugs, we found out some startling statistics:

- *We baby-boomer parents think we know about drugs, but there is a whole array of drugs we've never heard of or known about like GHB, Ecstasy, and Ketamine.*

- *"Club drugs" and raves are a whole new phenomenon.*

- *51% of high school students say it's pretty "easy" to get or buy drugs.*

- *"Club drugs" are often used in combination with methamphetamines, or "speed." And the result is often fatal.*

- *Kids as young as junior high and elementary school are aware of drugs, and the age at which they try drugs gets younger and younger.*

What we have found out has scared us. We're like so many parents out there. We send our children to school, we try to help our kids with homework, we love them, we get our babies inoculated when they're tiny so they don't catch fatal diseases, and we bring them to the pediatrician to get those dreaded "booster" shots when they get older. But how can we inoculate you kids against drugs? How can we fight this battle? Sometimes, we feel like we're fighting the biggest battle of our lives, but we have to—for Michael. We have to educate people—young people—to fight this battle with us. And we have to let parents know that though they may not be naïve, they may not really *know* the amount of peer pressure and the sheer availability of drugs out there. So many of us parents assume that because you kids all went to DARE classes in elementary school or because we're open with you or discuss drugs with you from time to time, that's enough. It isn't.

So as we continue to tell you our family's story, keep thinking about your family and your friends. And now, we're going to ask you to think about your grandparents. Yes, a lot of your grandparents are "out of touch." But for many of you, Grandma or Grandpa was always in your corner, maybe giving you special treats, letting you stay up late when you slept over their house, and in general spoiling you. Because, frankly, that's their job!

Michael's grandmother was that kind of wonderful person in his life. We thought, with horror, that terrible day that there was no way we could tell her over the phone about her precious grandson's death. So one of Brad's sisters went to her house in person.

Imagine this sweet woman opening her door, seeing her daughter standing there, and smiling, with that special "twinkle" many grandmothers have. She said, "To what do I owe this surprise visit?"

Now imagine. It's hard, we know... but Michael's aunt Jane had to tell her that Michael was dead. *This couldn't be!* That was his grandmother's reaction. There had to be some mistake. Michael's grandmother cried until her voice was so hoarse from crying she could barely speak. Bravely, then, she said she was flying down to Florida to be with us, along with Aunt Jane, Uncle Rex, and Aunt Judy. Families often come together in times of tragedy. What a horrible, lonely, frightening airplane ride that must have been.

We keep saying, in this book, "imagine." Imagine who you would leave behind. Imagine your father finding you. Imagine your mother finding you. Imagine leaving your friends. Imagine your grandmother's grief. That's a pretty tricky word, "imagine." Because maybe it seems far-off and dreamy. Maybe it seems like it could never happen to you... that it's just something to "imagine." To make up in your head.

Unfortunately, we can't "imagine" this away. Neither can Michael's grandmother, his friends, his classmates, and his teachers. We know what we have been through isn't rare. We wish it was, but we're learning as we speak to schools across the country (we're at 250,000 students spoken to and counting!) that we're not the only ones. Every time we speak at a school, when we get home, our website (www.michaelsmessage.org) is literally flooded with e-mails from kids who tell us their stories of experiences with drugs—whether themselves, their families, siblings, or friends. It's heartrending.

So we ask you one more time to imagine. Imagine who you would leave behind. And we ask you to remember: Just one "high" could prove fatal, no matter how careful you think you're being.

Imagine.

Michael: Who Would You Leave Behind?

Chapter Three

The Circle Of Life

No, we're not talking about a *Lion King* song. Well... we are a little bit. That movie most of you saw as kids or watched on video with your little brothers and sisters is about how in the jungle, there is a circle of life. Some creatures' die, some live, some grow old. New babies come each spring, and even if old members of the lion's pride have died, new cubs come along to take their place. This is the way it's supposed to be. It's the circle of life.

Parents are not supposed to bury their children. It isn't just a tragedy... it literally goes against the circle of life. Children are supposed to grow up and move on to happy and successful lives on their own. Many will marry and have children. They will create a new family, a new "lion's pride." They will find love and laughter as their own little ones teach them about life and the love a parent has for a child. Then later, much later, their parents will eventually die.

That is the circle of life. They will be sad, and they will grieve, but in the faces of grandchildren and great-grandchildren, most of us see that the circle of life indeed goes on. But not for us.

The day of Michaels' funeral was surreal. Not only was Michael gone... this just wasn't supposed to happen. This wasn't how life is supposed to be. We're not supposed to travel around talking to schools about our son, who has died. That's not the way life is. The circle for us has been broken.

Sometimes, tragically, life does have a way of defying the circle of life. Children sometimes die. They can contract cancer or leukemia. They might be involved in a car accident. For us, one of the hardest things about Michael's death was that it was so preventable. If only he had refused those drugs. If only someone hadn't *offered* them. If only drugs weren't so available to young people. If only.... That became our circle of life. Questions and what if's circling around and around and around in our heads and our hearts.

The days after Michael's death played out like a horrible nightmare we couldn't wake ourselves up from. Sometimes, almost like a mirage, when morning dawned, for a brief moment, we would feel a glimmer of hope... that it had all been a dream, but then the crushing reality of having to bury our son would nearly suffocate us with grief.

When the police came, our privacy walked out the door. When someone dies in your home, there must be an investigation. Three officers, all of them fathers and saddened by what we had to face, came to the house. An ambulance waited in the driveway to take his body away. It all seemed so cold. Almost like a movie. Like it was happening to someone else. Neighbors stood in their driveway, the curiosity seekers clustered around our home. *What happened?* They all wondered. But then the news spread like wildfire.

The police had to ask us painful questions and a cloud of suspicion hung over us. We wondered, in the back of our minds, what these policemen thought. Did anyone blame us? Did they really think somehow we were involved in our son's death? Did they look at us in a different way because of what had happened in our house, right under our very roof?

Worse, an officer came in with a video camera and was required to film our whole house. He wandered through our house videoing everything, even pointing the camera *right at us*, filming us in our most private moment, sobbing on the couch, both of us in our pajamas and bedclothes.

Next the officers went into Michael's room and searched it. There was no privacy. Just men going through his things, looking at everything, opening every drawer, upsetting the order in that room. And all this while Michael's body just lay there on the bed.

After about four hours, an officer approached us and told us that because Michael was young and healthy, with no obvious reason for his death, an autopsy would have to be performed. This was too much for Debbie to bear. She broke down even more, imagining our son's body being cut up.

Our daughter, Eliese, just graduated from nursing school, quietly took in the horrifying sight of her brother being carried out in a body bag, being taken away from us and our home for an autopsy. The coldness of this broke our hearts yet again.

Yet as horrible as this drama of dealing with the police was, we still had to plan a funeral—something we never could have imagined *ever*. We wanted Michael's funeral to reflect who he was. He attended a karate school, and he was very dedicated to the martial arts. We selected members of the karate school to be his pallbearers—to carry his casket. We buried him with his medals.

We're sure the pallbearers, Michael's friends, will never forget their grim task. They had just begun their teenage lives, and we're sure they had imagined many wonderful times ahead with their buddy, Michael. They carried the casket from the hearse to the gravesite. We had watched as, earlier, the funeral home director had shut Michael's casket for the last time. As parents, we would have traded places with our boy in an instant. All we could think was he was alone in that casket, and we were alone at the graveside. How would we ever go on? The circle of life had been broken. Something had gone tragically awry.

The day we buried Michael was chilly. But the real chill was in our hearts. Dirt was thrown on top of the casket. It's usual at a funeral to quote the Bible. The preacher or minister might say, "Ashes to ashes, dust to dust." It's one of those expressions that you don't really think about too much, but that day, there was Michael, our Michael, going into the Earth, returning to dust. It was too much to bear.

After the funeral, our lives were still turned upside down. How do you wander through your house, the house filled with memories and usually echoing with the voices of young people—Michael and his friends—and now so painfully quiet? Its silence tormented us. We couldn't bear to eat at the kitchen table because usually it was the three of us. Now we were alone, just us two. The living room was a place where we watched sports together, or laughed as we threw Christmas parties or had friends over. Now instead of the rings of laughter, one or the other of us would start to sob. The silence closed in around us.

Christmas came that year. How do you even get out of bed, let alone drag down Christmas ornaments from the attic? Michael, like all kids, loved the holidays. As our youngest child, we spoiled him—and now we're sure glad we did. We strived to make each Christmas memorable for him. But we no longer had a reason to celebrate this sacred holiday. We no longer had a reason to celebrate anything.

His older sister Eliese's son, Shawn, our grandson, missed his "Uncle Michael." It seemed like everywhere we looked, every person we dealt with, was touched forever by the tragedy. Eliese was ten years older than Michael, so he had been almost like her baby, too.

Though we have a close-knit extended family, it became too painful for us to all be together. Each of us isolated in our own way. We didn't want to go to gatherings of cousins and aunts and uncles. It was too obvious that someone was missing. When we were all together, we felt a tangible emptiness even more than when we were alone. Rather than comforting each other, it made things worse. So we kept to ourselves, alone in the house. We saw no one but each other.

We searched for a reason to go on. Depression greeted us when we woke up each day, and filled our home and our heart like a mist or a fog. We couldn't see through it or past it; we lived enveloped by it. The fog was so heavy we could barely see each other, yet we did cling to each other for comfort.

We eventually decided to sell our house. Though some complicated real estate happenings occurred, we did sell the home where Michael died. We packed up our things, thinking if we left that house, maybe we could breathe again, free from the fog. But the fog of grief followed us.

We saw a psychologist. We prayed. We struggled. Yet the pain remained. It became very clear to us that because this circle of life had been broken, we had no meaning to our lives. How could our life have meaning? All we had worked for and all we had dreamed was about the circle of life one day extending with our son. We would grow old and have our grandkids around. We would spoil those grandkids and love whatever girl Michael chose to be his wife as if she was our own daughter. What now?

Yet as time wore on, many mysterious and, in their own way, miraculous and wonderful, events would occur. We would have dreams that led us to establish Michael's Message. We would never, ever be able to fix the circle of life, as it had been irretrievably broken. But we would discover that, through our educating kids about the dangers of drugs, through feeling as if our lives still had a purpose, and a purpose that was greater than ourselves and was committed to our son's memory, that we could live.

The fog hasn't left us. The way we think of it is like the savannahs where the lions hunt. In the morning, there is a mist. But the sun rises and burns off that mist and all the living creatures are there, visible, in the bright sun of the African day. But the next morning, the mist will be there again. It's always there. Our grief hasn't left us. We can see clearly enough now that we have a purpose, but it's still there each morning, clouding the way just a bit. Yet Michael's Message is the sun that burns off the mist and lets us accomplish our goals each day.

Michael: Who Would You Leave Behind?

Chapter Four

A Victory

You could hear a pin drop.

Actually, from where we stood, we felt like we could hear the beating hearts of five hundred students out in the audience listening to us.

We could hear the sniffling of young girls—and guys—crying.

Yet up until two years ago, neither of us had ever made a public presentation or a speech in our lives. We're not famous. Unless you're one of the 250,000 or so students who have seen us speak or you have seen us testify to Congress, or seen our pictures and story on television or in the newspaper, you wouldn't know us. What we look like is a typical Mom and Dad. Two parents.

And we are.

We have two children. Or, actually, we guess it's more correct to say we *had* two children. One of our kids, Michael, died of a drug overdose, and though we feel his presence every minute of every day, we don't actually have the wonderful gift of having him here, with us, on earth. And we guess that's how it is we came to talk to this group of 500 high school kids.

What do we say?

Surprisingly, though the words and our story are sad, the words come, almost as if Michael is whispering them to us. First Debbie speaks. She talks about drugs and she has a long list of information and warnings. She educates students and parents about the dangers of illicit drugs as well as prescription drugs.

Did you know GHB has poisonous ingredients like acid and Drano?

Did you know that every year kids die instantly from trying Ecstasy and GHB? These aren't "harmless club drugs."

Do you know the signs of an overdose?

Do you know that if you put your drink down at a party, and it has left your possession, that you must think of that drink as trash—because GHB and other drugs are odorless and colorless and you could be slipped drugs rendering you unconscious or worse?

Debbie talks for about twenty minutes. Then it's Brad's turn.

This is usually when kids start to cry. It's not that we try to intentionally make anyone cry. We don't. But Brad shares what it was like as a parent to have to pick out a coffin for his son. What it was like to touch Michael's hair for the last time. What it was like to watch the coffin close and know his son was being buried. What it was like, before all that, to be a father to Michael. What it was like to find his body the morning after his accidental overdose.

It's exhausting. We spend our days going to school after school telling our story. We're tired. We're often broke. But we don't do this to make money or to have fun. We do it to save lives.

So on this day, speaking to 500 kids, we hear the crying. We finished speaking. We got a standing ovation. Then we went about the business of packing up. And then a small miracle happened.

Two high school girls approached us, crying. They seemed shy, unsure of what to say. We hugged them, and then they told us: "We have to thank you… we were going to a party tomorrow night, and we were going to try Ecstasy. We're not going to anymore. Thanks to you. We made a pact that we're not going to do drugs. It's not worth it."

We hugged them again and told them how relieved and happy we were. Perhaps they were two lives we have just saved. Later, long after the auditorium was dark, long after we packed up our pamphlets and information, we held hands. Today was a good day in our fight against drugs. Today, we won.

Michael: Who Would You Leave Behind?

Chapter Five

Lonely Holidays

Mother's Day used to be a day Debbie loved. All mothers look forward to that special day each year when your kids bring you breakfast in bed and homemade cards manufactured with love. But the first Mother's Day after Michael's death was devastating. She recalled the hour and the minute Michael came into this world, and at the same time felt the pain of his absence. The pain and sorrow was so overwhelming, that it really felt like we had the flu—our emotional and mental anguish became a physical pain.

We found life very difficult at this time in our lives. We had just suffered through our first Mother's Day without our son. This year we didn't have a family gathering or family dinner. We spent time standing at Michael's grave.

But as the year wore on, it wasn't like it got any easier. Mother's Day passed and then, before we knew it, it was Father's Day. We decided to get away and drive over to Lake Okeechobee—this is a huge lake in Florida and very pretty country. We were very quiet all the way there. As usual, there were times when both of us just had tears streaming down our faces. Part of us actually wondered if we would ever cry ourselves out. But we've come to find that the loss of a child is so intense and so unnatural in the grand scheme of the universe, that the reservoir of grief is bottomless.

Eventually, that first Father's Day, we stopped to eat at a truck stop. While waiting for Debbie in the restroom, Brad glanced to his left where there was a rack of Father's Day cards. He was led to read what he could see of two of the front of the cards. In truth, he wanted to ignore the cards, but there seemed to be a force there and Brad could see Michael. Michael was in front of him, above him, but his face was even with Brad's, with his beautiful smile. For that moment, the spirit of Michael was real, but he was gone just as fast as he arrived. Brad found himself sitting at the table, thinking of what just happened. He had to fight back tears while he ate. This was Michael's way of giving me Brad a Father's Day card. Oh what a wonderful gift!

This experience Brad had that sad yet wonderful day reassures us that we still receive Michael's love and his tender touch from the spirit world. Michael is still alive, just in a different place, and one day we know we will all be together again.

The year went on. Michael's 16th birthday loomed. How would your Mom, Dad, sisters, and brothers celebrate your birthday if you were to die? Would your mom want to bake or buy your favorite cake? Michael's mom was very quiet that day. You could almost hear her thinking. Parents always imagine the perfect birthday for their sixteen- year-old. It's a special birthday, a time when kids edge still closer to adulthood. Our dreams, Michael's wishes, were all blown away by a wrong choice.

We didn't have cake on his special day. No laughter, no excitement, and no presents. We only felt sadness and depression. We stood at his grave, eyes filled with tears. Instead of having a party, celebrating Michael's birthday, we sat down to the table with a setting for two. Michael's empty chair was staring us in the face. This caused us to have so much pain, sorrow, and emptiness in our mind, heart, and souls.

We started out the prayer before our meal asking God to tell Michael happy birthday. We stopped. We both started crying. We suddenly ended the prayer by saying amen. Nothing more was said. We struggled to finish our dinner. We slept very little that night.

The year wore on. Nine months after we lost Michael, we still found it hard to sit at the same dinner table to eat our evening meal. When it had been nine months since the tragedy that forever changed our lives, we found ourselves five months behind on one mortgage, and four months behind on the other mortgage. We just were so incapacitated by grief that we neglected the basic things in life— paying bills, balancing a checkbook. We couldn't work. We couldn't function. It was as if we were continually in a fog.

We seemed to be alone, as our friends stopped visiting. They didn't know what to say and felt uneasy. We had some members of the family that did not come around after Michael's funeral. We didn't go to their house nor did they visit us. Looking back at it now, we feel they felt too uncomfortable to come. They couldn't deal with the pain we faced. Finally enough time had gone by, which gave us all some healing. We were able to examine the tragedy in our minds. We were starting to put the pieces together, to look at what happened. We knew we could never "move on." That wasn't possible. But we started to have the fog lift. We were able to go to the store and look at our finances, and pay our bills.

Still, we faced the loss of our house. We had built it. Michael's mother made it into a beautiful home. I call it a home, because it was just full of happiness and laughter when Michael was alive. Michael and his friends raided the refrigerator each day after school. But after Michael died, it was no longer a home. It was a house filled with sadness and depression. We wanted out of this house, to get away from the pain and hurt. We sold our boat. We had taken Michael and his friends out on the boat. Taught him to drive the boat, ski, and tube. Michael and his friends camped on the islands. After Michael's death, we took the boat out, but we got no enjoyment out of it. All of the laughter was gone.

As I said earlier, we no longer enjoyed life. We wanted to leave this tragedy behind and start fresh in a new house. But unbeknownst to us, our path was going to change.

Chapter Six

Communication From Beyond

Michael's spirit and God gave us new direction, a new meaning for our lives. We believe Michael found a way to communicate with us that it was okay for us to try to live our lives positively—we didn't need to remain in a pit of grief.

As we look back and remember our son trying to communicate with us, we experienced poltergeist activity in the house right after Michael died. One night we were all in the house, Brad was in the living room watching TV, Debbie and some family members were in the office on the computer. All of a sudden, we heard this loud crash and glass breaking. Brad hesitated a moment to get out of his chair to look, because the crash was so loud, he thought maybe one of our beautiful oak cabinets had fallen off the wall and glass would be everywhere. By the time Brad got out of his chair, Debbie and the others were standing at the entrance to the kitchen with horrified looks on their faces, eyes bugged out, and in unison we all yelled "**MICHAEL**!"

The kitchen cabinets were all still intact, but what was on the floor were splintered pieces of glass. It was a thick crystal ashtray that had belonged to Debbie's grandmother. The ashtray had been sitting on top of the microwave, which was shoved back in the corner of the kitchen. There were probably sixteen to twenty inches of space in front of the microwave to prepare foods before putting them in to cook. Eerily, for this ashtray to fall off, it would have had to fall on the countertop and then to the floor. We found most of the broken ashtray on the opposite side of the room as if it had been thrown very hard. This was only the beginning of our "poltergeist activities." (A poltergeist is a ghost or spirit, which is said to manifest its presence by noises, knockings, and other disturbances.) We believe the spirit of Michael has taken glasses out of the cabinet, turned lights on and off, and moved items around the house. Michael's favorite pastime seems to be to drop pennies around the house.

Realizing that our son was alive in the spirit world made our lives even more difficult. Did he need Dad's help? His mother's love? We weren't yet sure.

Perhaps in an attempt to understand what was happening, we went to a psychic. We first must explain. We think there are psychics who are devoted to their work here on this planet, and then there are selfish individuals taking advantage and misinterpreting and damaging the true work. It's like buying a car; there are a lot of good ones out there to purchase and some are lemons. If someone is seeking a lot of money find a psychic that is just as good and one you can afford. Listen to your gut instinct.

A friend told us about this psychic, and for two months we dealt with the thought of seeking help from this human being. Brad had been brought up in a religion that claimed this is the devil's work. Now, when he looks back on these teachings, he thinks it was wrong. Still, we were slow seeking this new information. Like many people, we had been left by our upbringing with a vision of a punishing God. We often wonder if this is why people seek drugs to reach the unknown euphoria, ecstasy the ultimate feeling of the great energy of universal love.

Our inner voices finally won after two months, and we decided to seek communication from the other side. We didn't tell anyone we were going. We went to the psychic bookstore and made an appointment. The owner of the store asked the nature of our endeavor. We simply replied we would like to talk to some loved ones from the other side.

Her reply was, "I think Elka would be best for the job." Elka came to the bookstore on Wednesday, but the Wednesday coming up was marked "off." We had to schedule for the following week. We thought about our appointment as we waited, every day hoping we would be able to communicate with our beloved departed son Michael.

Wednesday finally arrived. We had other business in town that day so we left our home early that morning. We had forgotten the exact time we were to be there, so we arrived early. When we walked in the bookstore we reminded the store owner that we were there for a reading with Elka. Her reply was, "Oh, you didn't get my message on your machine." When we had made the appointment, we had only given our first name and phone number (which is unlisted), so we knew they couldn't receive any information about us by going this route.

Unfortunately, we were told that Elka was sick with the flu, and she wouldn't be doing any readings that day. Our mouths fell wide open, and our hearts ached with disappointment. We almost took this as an omen; this was not to be. We agreed to make another appointment. We had to wait another week, another week of anxiety, wondering if this woman was just going to take our money—if she was a charlatan.

The long week had finally passed. We entered this small bookstore. A woman with a foreign accent greeted us. Shaking our hands, she said, "Come, follow me, I am Elka." This woman began to explain how sorry she was that she was unable to keep our first appointment. As she spoke, we were filled with worry—her accent was quite thick, and we feared we wouldn't be able to understand her.

We sat down at this table in a small room with furnishings and chairs stacked on one side. We learned later that this room was where they held group meditation meetings. Elka asked each of us to take a penny, flip it into the air three times and let it land on the table. I believe she asked of our birth dates, too. She asked what we were seeking. We told her we were there to communicate with loved ones on the other side. We didn't say anything about Michael. After flipping the penny, she seemed to cipher numbers on a piece of paper.

Elka was addressing Debbie, looking over Debbie's head. She said, "Debbie, I believe I have your dad here wanting to talk with you. He says his name is John, but he was also called Jack." This was true—that was her father's name. Our hearts began to pound a mile a minute, all the while, wanting to talk to Michael. Would Debbie's dad bring a message from Michael? He made a statement that his time here on the earth plane wasn't very long, that he was sick a lot. That he was here with us today to thank Debbie for being so caring and understanding to pitch in with the needs of the family.

Debbie began to cry. Wiping tears from her face she explained to Elka that she went to work at a very young age and gave her entire paycheck to her mother each week. Debbie told of working at the local drugstore starting at age fifteen. Debbie chose to put her college education on the back burner so that she could help her family with financial support and moral support.

Elka then spoke of Debbie's dad being an avid hunter and fisherman, which was very much the truth. We watched this truth unfold right before our eyes. My hands began to sweat from anticipation and excitement.

Elka shared that there were many spirits here today to visit with us. We began to look around the room as if we would see a ghost at any second. We had mixed feelings. On the one hand, we hoped to see something tangible, and at the same time we were scared that we would. If we did, what would we do?

Elka kept looking above us, as if she could see these spirits, our loved ones. She said, "There is a young man, a boy here that wants to talk with you.... He says his name is Mika or Mida. I can't understand him; he is speaking too fast. He hasn't been over on the other side for very long, I know this because he is speaking so fast. You are going to have to help me with his name." With our hearts pounding, and our minds running rapidly, we both echoed "Michael" back to her. She said, "Yes, he says 'yes.' He is very excited to be here. This is your son correct?"

We nodded.

"Yes, he is sorry it was an accident. He wasn't supposed to go like this."

His mother began to cry.

Elka said, "He is saying it had something to do with drugs. He wasn't aware, seemed like that day was a roller coaster, it kept going faster and faster and he couldn't get off. He keeps saying he's very sorry, he didn't know."

We became comfortable with this communication, so we began to ask Michael questions directly to him instead of asking Elka to ask him. He could hear the questions from us; Elka didn't have to translate it to him, although we couldn't hear him or see him. Elka would reiterate what Michael was sharing. During this time, Elka's accent seemed to dissolve so we could clearly understand her.

We asked Michael about his death, what he had experienced. Elka shared with us that he turned away—he didn't want to talk about it. It was too painful yet. We shared a few other things, and then Elka expressed that Michael was standing next to me. "He is standing next to you now, Dad. He is handing something to you saying, thank you. It is something you wear around your neck, but it is not a necklace, he is saying you buried these with him. He is giving these back to you dad and saying thanks." Elka told us she didn't know what they were, but she drew us a picture of what he was handing me.

This was her drawing. We buried Michael with his karate medallions from tournaments. This brought tears to our eyes. Brad had spent so much time with him in karate. The trips to class three times a week, the tournaments, encouraging Michael when he felt his energy waning and wanted to quit. But Michael did get his black belt and many, many trophies. He made his dad scream with joy many, many times. Thank you my son for all of those memories!

Elka also shared with us that she saw a vision of Debbie and I standing before large groups of people speaking. She also expressed that she was shown lots of pages, a book. Elka told us that we would be writing a book. She couldn't explain about the two of us standing before large crowds of people. We now understand what this vision was all about. Only later would Michael's dream give us direction of speaking before people.

Michael shared more information with us, and this reading had gone on for a little over an hour. We were feeling really very tired. This kind of work drains the energy from the body. Elka told us he was walking away, that he must be finished. We both said, "Good-bye, we love you" in stereo.

We began to get up from our chairs, thanking Elka for the wonderful time we were able to spend with our son, Michael. At that very moment, Elka looked wide-eyed above our heads and behind us. She said, "Oh my! He is back, and he has brought a dog with him."

As Elka said he's back, and he's brought a dog with him, without thinking, Brad blurted out, "Oh yeah, what kind of dog?" Elka described our Ruthie-U-Gene to a tee. This was just some more confirmation that it was truly our son. Ruthie died one year to the month after Michael. Michael died October 2, 1998 and Ruthie-U-Gene died October 23, 1999.

The Story of One Family's Fight Against Drug Abuse

Chapter Seven

Peer Pressure

We must remember, Michael told Brad, "Dad, I have to say no every day!" Every day he saw another friend of his begin his or her start in drug activity. These kids thought they were old enough or smart enough, or had enough willpower, to be able to keep a handle on their experimenting.

The first demand of peer pressure that is put on every child is the cigarette. The tobacco industry makes their cancer sticks look so appealing. The thought and excitement of doing something wrong, behind their parents' backs gives them a feeling of independence, a feeling of being grown-up.

This behavior is the beginning of a cruel, vicious, and disappointing roller coaster for the teen, loved ones, and friends. Just like our son, the peer pressure he faced daily, finally broke his barrier down, until he gave in, smoked that first time and from there it continued to escalate. It was a cool thing, just like on the last day of his life, it was cool, all laughter. Today, Michael's mother and I continue to find it hard to laugh. We cry every day from a memory, or seeing a child that resembles Michael. The illegal drug industry is taking too many of our sons, daughters, mothers, and fathers.

We must recognize that evening, Michael's last evening, when his friend handed him GHB, his friend didn't say with a sad serious look on his face, *Michael be very careful this drug has killed*. No, it was all laughs and giggles, you got it, all right, let's do it, what a rush. It was a rush all right, a rush to ending a great life. How many times has this scenario happened throughout America? By sharing our experience, we hope it will help you to realize how important it is that you make the right choice, so your family won't have to endure the sorrow and pain our family suffers daily.

Telling Mom and Dad: Drugs At School

Our children come home from school, telling us, that they have to say no to drugs in school, or they are asked on the bus. They tell us that the peer pressure is horrendous. Does this mean when they refuse to take drugs they are rejected among their friends? Every time we have a discussion with students, when visiting schools, we are told of the enormous amount of peer pressure.

What are we to do about this stigma? It's this overwhelming thing called peer pressure. We have all heard of it. We need to make our schools safer, so our children will not have this pressure to do drugs. We will find ourselves spending immense sums of money. The first step is to get past the problem of denial.

We have to change the way we think of our drug problems in school. We need to realize that ALL of our schools have drugs in them. Our principals do not want their schools marked as "bad schools." We need a different attitude toward this major problem. We cannot depend on or expect our students to tell. This is just not going to happen. These students are scared of the thugs in their lives, just as many adults have to be aware of them in adult situations.

We felt like we no longer wanted to live after Michael's death. If we could only have made Michael's a safer world, a drug-free world. Now we realize this wasn't just *our* battle. It's *all of our* battle.

Someone once said to a friend of ours whose children all grew to adulthood, went to college, married happily, had children, "What did you do right so that none of your girls got into drugs?" The mother of these three now-grown women said, "My husband and I were *lucky.*" Unfortunately, great schools and great parents and great families have kids who get into drugs. Yes, sometimes it's a school in a rough neighborhood or a child from a broken family, but that's not always or even often the case. It is everywhere, and we all need to change this. *This* is what our society must strive to accomplish. Our kids must learn of the devastation drugs cause. Students should not have to worry every morning when they wake up, being concerned if they will have the strength to stay focused and refuse their friend when confronted to smoke their first joint, or cigarette. We have no choice but to make our schools a drug-free environment and campus.

Strategies

To make our schools safer for our children, we need more school resource officers on campus. Our suggestion is cameras installed on campus and more manpower. The drug dealer will be caught red-handed, and when caught, the punishment can and must be severe. Each case should be dealt with separately with different avenues to choose from.

Churches need to be more active with our schools. I don't mean to teach Bible verses, but many are just a phone call away, to come to schools to assist, stand in the halls or ride a bus home. This will have to be a select group. These will have to be personalities of leadership and strength, not hesitant to induce authority.

One school policy will be no sleeping, or lying of heads on the desk. This would be a trip to the office, where parents should be called in. Let the parents be aware of their child not getting enough sleep at night. Make the parents be responsible for their child.

School Policy and Parent Role: Parents Need Parenting Skills

We often hear of a school calling a parent to school to be told of a problem, and the child denies the accusation. The parent agrees with the child, calling the teacher or other person in authority a liar or they are mistaken. This is absurd. This is where we have to STOP—most teachers are dedicated to teaching and loving our children. That is why they become teachers. When this happens, a red flag should go up. This should tell us that this family is in need of assistance. There are special agencies that deal with this kind of situation. They should be called in to help correct the problem and assist the family. Teachers have told us about this problem, and it disturbs us. When this happens, the child thinks he has won, but when you sit back and look at the whole situation, everybody loses.

Teachers Need Help!

They are one of our biggest assets. We need to get a message to trust and help our teachers. The teacher loses control of the student, the student loses respect for the teacher, and the problem just escalates. Teachers lose interest and start going through the motions of their job. This is one of many reasons we have students making A's and B's in their early years of school, and getting discouraged and dropping out when they reach high school.

We used to hear about the student who was a slow learner, or a dysfunctional child dropping out of school. Our honor students are dropping out and, going to community colleges to get their GED's. What kind of world do we live in? When our children choose to drop out of school, because of the drug and violent atmosphere they are forced to face each and every day.

Michael: Who Would You Leave Behind?

Chapter Eight

Michael's Dream

We had suffered through our second Christmas and all the holidays that are included in our second year without Michael. We continued to search ourselves, and we had a hunger. What are we to do with the rest of our lives? Deb and I seemed to be drifting further apart from one another. We were shutting down. We didn't fight with each other, nor did we point the finger, accusing each other for Michael's demise. We were both constantly lost in our thoughts with a great deal of misery and depression hovering over our heads every day. We felt very old, and every day we woke up Michael's death was there as soon as we opened our eyes. This caused us to feel sick, like a flu symptom.

When you experience a great loss like that, it almost seems like a dream. You go to sleep with depression crushing your chest, and you wake up and for a tiny split-second, you think that perhaps you imagined it all. Then the reality hurtles at you.

It wasn't a dream. It wasn't a nightmare. Your child is really gone. You don't want to face another day.

It was at this time that Michael came to Brad in a dream. We both had been waiting and wanting this to happen. This dream, it seemed to be so real and very clear. Although Brad can only remember the message, he can clearly remember Michael standing in front of him, and he clearly remembers Michael's handsome face.

In Brad's dream, Michael was standing in front of him and as their eyes met, Brad could see his beautiful smile, but he knew Michael was dead in his dream. Brad wanted to put his arms around Michael to hold and comfort him, but he could tell he wasn't to do that. Brad could sense Michael had a very short time with him. Michael seemed to be really pressed for time. Brad's heart was pounding, and he was so full of excitement. Brad remembers Michael holding both of his hands. That seemed to settle Brad down a little, gathering his composure, still nervous or anxious. Michael looked at him and said, *"Dad, it is a sin to destroy the body like I have done. To make things right where I am at, I need to ask you and mother to go out and tell my friends and my generation of people my story, our tragedy. Dad you don't have a clue of the drug activity that goes on in my generation."*

This is what Brad remembers of the dream. He woke the next morning and shared the dream with Debbie. She was excited, but also hurt, or disappointed because Michael didn't come to her. The request he was asking of us, literally frightened us both. Brad's inner thought, or inner voice, was telling and showing him that we were to travel to schools and share Michael's story.

Brad dealt with this inner voice asking him about this mission every morning when he woke up. Asking when we were going to do this. Debbie and I seemed to stop healing. Brad searched his soul, asking God how could we possibly achieve this assignment. Because Brad had suffered a closed brain injury years before, he was not able to remember things easily. A loud noise, or just a door opening could cause him to loose his concentration. Therefore, how could we accomplish such a large task? *Speak* to large crowds? The thought was terrifying. Brad said, "God, I don't have the money or the means to travel and do this kind of work." God repeatedly told Brad to just do it! *Do not worry about the moneys, just have faith and believe in me.* In his prayers, Brad said, "God, sometimes I can't even remember my wife's name." God said again, *Just do it!*

After Michael's dream, we had a spiritual awakening. We began to go to meditation class once a week on Thursday evening. The people in the class had balance in their lives, had a lot of love and respect for other people.

As a couple, we pondered on this large emotional task for two months. We both were crying every day, dealing with a lot of depression. A little over two-months after the dream, or Michael's contact, Deb told Brad she was going to town. On this day God and the spirits were working on Brad's heart. A thought came to him. This thought was to make the first step toward our assignment. This inner voice told Brad to pick up the phone and call St. Andrews, where Michael had attended elementary school. This inner voice told Brad to call the principal and make an appointment for us to tell Michael's story.

It is amazing how the spirits work. Brad was shaking, very nervous. He made the call hoping the principal wouldn't be available. To Brad's surprise, she was able to talk with him right there and then. Brad explained our desire to do this kind of work. That wonderful principal didn't give Brad a chance to change his mind. We had a speaking engagement March 16th, 2000.

Debbie came home from town. When Brad told her what had happened, we wished we had a camera to take a picture. The look I received was priceless. Where had Debbie been that day? She was at the same school talking with the priest. That day Debbie was at one of her all-time lows. So while Brad was making arrangements, she was there, at the school. Brad had no idea. It is astonishing how God and the spirits work.

We prayed and got closer to God than we had ever been before. We were not going to stand before the students by ourselves. God never leaves us standing alone. He is always right there ready to pick us up when we stumble. We could never really come up with a speech, no matter how hard we tried. March 16th arrived, and we still had nothing written. We dressed looking very professional and as we drove to Michael's school we prayed all the way there. God, please give us the power to make a difference in the lives of all who will hear "Michael's Message."

Ladies are always first, so Debbie stood before the students holding back tears and she began. "We are not here to lecture or accuse you of being bad kids, nor are we here to scare you. We are here to share with you our tragedy of losing a good kid to drugs."

Michael's Message is a very informative, factual, emotional and powerful message that comes from the heart. Michael's Message has developed into a nonprofit corporation. Michael's message is our lives. The first year we were honored to share Michael's Message before the United States Congress traveling to Washington, D.C., visiting the capital mall, seeing the monuments. This was a lot of enjoyment. In our first year, we shared our drug awareness program with over 35,000 students! We have gone to churches, prisons, and many schools in our home state of Florida. We have had the privilege of having our story published in many newspapers and have been on different TV programs and on the evening news. We plan to take our program nationwide.

We endure sorrow and cry often still missing our beautiful son. Now we are happy to share that we do have meaning in our lives. We live Michael's Message. It is time-consuming, requires a lot of devotion, and we love every minute of it. We feel by sharing Michael's message we are able to prevent another family from experiencing a tragedy such as ours. The students walk away with a new awareness about how damaging drugs are and how important an individual choice is. Students are aware of the pain they could cause their family and loved ones from a wrong choice. As time passes we continue to grow and we become stronger with spirits help. We do have happiness in our lives but there is not a day that goes by that we do not miss our son.

Michael: Who Would You Leave Behind?

Chapter Nine

Living The Dream

Debbie and I began living Michael's dream. We shared our experience of losing a child to drugs with our local schools. The news began to travel that there was a new drug awareness program called Michael's Message, and the students walked away with a better understanding of how important it is to make the right choices in their lives. Students learn that the choices they make affect their mother, father, sisters, brothers, grandparents, and all of their friends. The students' walk away from our program understanding that a wrong choice made by themselves and friends can affect their school, their whole community.

Every family in America has a story to share about the disappointment and devastation drugs have caused. This often starts from friends and a wrong choice, the choice of finally giving in and saying yes.

Surviving Our Third Christmas Without Michael
A Sign Of Healing

As I (Brad) write this, Michael died two years ago this past October 2nd. Though it has been two years, this will be our third Christmas. Michael's mother was always big on decorating the house for Christmas, or any other holiday, Thanksgiving, Halloween, Easter and etc. Since Michael's death, this procedure has stopped. I myself used to enjoy putting up the lights outside. Michael would always help us, climbing up into the attic every year getting lights and decorations down from storage.

The excitement that holidays bring just seemed to bypass us, bringing sadness and depression. This is our third Christmas without our beloved son. We were at the Cracker Barrel restaurant with our grandson heading over to the Indian Reservation for a rodeo.

When we were pulling up to the Cracker Barrel, we noticed they were having a sidewalk sale. This excited Michael's mother, she had a hard time walking on into the store. The store was very busy people wanting some good cooked food. We were seated, waiting for our waitress. Our grandson Shawn wanted to play a game of checkers with his Grandpa while we waited for our food. This was the only thing on his young mind. "Come on Grandpa, let's go play," this is what we heard breaking in our conversation. This restaurant takes you back in time. Rocking chairs lined up on the front porch to sit and enjoy the day or play a good old-fashioned game of checkers.

We ordered our food, and then up from the table we all sprang. Debbie headed for the sidewalk sale, Shawn and I to the checkerboard table. Shawn was getting the best of his grandpa when Debbie came up telling me of the ceramic Christmas villages for sale. There was one she wanted to buy. This was the first interest in wanting to buy any Christmas decorations since Michael's death.

She came to me wanting my approval to buy this decoration for Christmas. I just about fell out of my chair, but I was careful with my response. I gave her my approval in a gentle way, not wanting to upset her or ruin that moment. I'm very thankful that we both have that kind of respect for each other's feelings.

Debbie was busy out front purchasing this little village at the same time our food was being placed on the table. Our checker game was coming to an end. I believe Shawn had more kings than I did. Shawn and I left our game and went to the table to say grace. But Grandma wasn't there.

We started our meal, just the two of us, staring at Grandma's eggs knowing they were getting colder by the second. I ask Shawn to go fetch Grandma. I was a little annoyed. Shawn brought Grandma back to the table. Michael's mother, Shawn's grandmother, was full of excitement her eyes had that twinkle in them. She had bought three large bags full of Christmas decorations. Debbie was so full of excitement I could hardly believe what my eyes were seeing.

For the first time I was seeing the excitement I had always seen at Christmas time. I looked deep into her face I could see the excitement and happiness, her beautiful smile the one I had often seen when Michael had made her proud and happy. Her face was gleaming, full of life and happiness.

As we finished our meal, we decided that she would pay the bill, and I would carry the packages of happiness and excitement out to the van. As I walked through the store, I was fighting back tears, but I was losing the battle. I could feel these tears running down my face, and I wanted to be out of the store. I tried to hide my face racing to the back of the van.

I had experienced the first signs of healing. The wonderful joy of feeling the excitement of the Christmas holiday, this I thought was lost forever. I had such a joyous feeling seeing Michael's mother, my wife, with so much excitement of the Christmas holiday.

As I was at the back of the van packing our bags of happiness away, I wiped my tears and put on my sunglasses. Debbie was finished paying for breakfast, and she walked up to me behind the van looking at me, asking me if I was all right, and looking my face over. I shrugged and said, "Sure I'm all right." She was concerned I was having a moment. We have them on a daily basis. It is amazing to see achievements and signs of healing. I believe in time we will have our lives back, but there will always be that empty void. I hope and pray as each Christmas comes it will get a little better each year. These Christmas Villages weren't put on display this year, our third Christmas, they stayed in the sacks we bought them in, still no tree this year, maybe next year. But we were making some progress in our healing.

Chapter Ten

Mary, the Cocaine Addict

We have listened to drug users or drug-addicted people. Each one of these souls has a family. These addicts are someone's child, brother, sister, and maybe even a father or mother themselves. These individuals have abused their loved ones in many ways, and yet they seem to be powerless in the grips of the demons of drugs.

This one addict, we'll call Mary. Mary came from a family of great respect and character. Her mother and father own their business and are very successful. Mary wasn't the only child—she had the privilege of having sisters. Mary and her sisters are very pretty, and when they were in high school they were very popular and well liked by their classmates. Mary and her sisters had the honor and privilege of being on the cheerleading team.

Mary made bad choices throughout her young adult life. Mary was introduced to pot or marijuana. This was the start of Mary's life with drugs. In time, Mary had more choices to make. When she started smoking pot she knew that it was wrong. This seemed to put excitement in her life. She had to hide this activity from her loved ones. This brought her excitement and a new challenge in her life. To keep this activity from people became a game to her. Mary learned she could do this and keep up with most of her responsibilities. As time passed she began to think it was all right to take pills to keep her awake for school.

Mary was introduced to a drug from a dear friend of hers. This drug she was introduced to was crack cocaine known as "Rocks." Mary loved this high, and she decided this would be a weekend thing. But Mary became a slave to this drug. This drug actually talked to her in her mind like a voice or a demon.

This voice took over Mary's life. This crack cocaine addiction or voice would tell Mary it was time to feed her body. Mary began losing friends; she was seen in places where most people wouldn't want to be. This addiction or voice grew with such momentum, it was like a train going at full speed and running out of track, in her case money.

Mary began to look at life differently. She began to think people were against her. The friends she once had no longer called. This drug or voice became more and more demanding. This drug voice would tell her "I need to be fed" meaning more crack cocaine. Mary had asked her mother and father for so much that the money purse was now being refused. Mary and her drug voice perceived this "no" as *you don't love me; you don't care what happens to me.* This made her mother, father, and her family the "Enemy." They didn't love her—that was her thinking.

Mary lowered her moral standards. To feed her addiction, the voice told Mary to steal. She lowered her standards again by selling her body. Mary was in big trouble now. She had lost all self-respect and self-esteem, and all of her friends had structure to their lives. Her friends were doing the things that set them up for success in life. Preparing for college, enjoying movies and the mall, and family activities, sports. But not Mary. Her entire world was Rocks.

Mary had made life so unbearable for everyone at home she stormed out of the house, swearing she would never be back. Her mother and father's hearts were crushed. They had no idea what to do. They found they loved her as a daughter, but despised her as a human being. How had this happened to their Mary? Her sisters were devastated.

Mary and her addiction or demon finally found they were in need of more crack cocaine. The voice told Mary to go back home while everyone else was gone for the day, while they were all at work. Mary went home and loaded up the family TV and other household items to sell.

Her mother and father come home from a stressful day to find they had no TV to watch the evening news or Monday Night Football. Worse, they had a sinking feeling they knew who did this. Mary's family was crushed again by her actions. They discussed the matter and decided to call the police. The police advised them to have her arrested. They were informed if they pressed charges, more than likely the judge would sentence her to a drug treatment center to help her get off of these drugs. Her parents could not get themselves to do this. Mary would have a criminal record. They did agree to have an order drawn up so Mary would not be permitted on the premises. Her mother cried a river of tears asking where she went wrong. Mary's mother blamed herself for Mary's actions.

A few days later, Mary was caught shoplifting. By now, she was owned by a pimp who bailed her out of jail. Her pimp beat her severely for getting caught shoplifting and costing him money. That night Mary was out selling her body for $20. Mary had fallen a long way from being a cheerleader, a popular girl in school.

Mary has been in and out of rehab centers many times. *We have been told by many that this drug crack cocaine is so addicting that the voice is real in the person's head.* The last time we saw Mary she was standing on a corner of U.S. #1. She looked as if she only weighed 90 pounds. Mary stood there as we drove by, with her thumb in the air. Looking for a ride. Looking for a customer.

Chapter Eleven

The Little College Student and Waitress

We were in Gainesville to speak at the University of Florida. We were scheduled to speak at 8:00 that evening. The evening engagements always seem to worry us, wondering if we will have a large audience. I remember this evening we stood before 500 students.

We decided we would have dinner, since our presentation was scheduled for later in the evening. We knew by the time we tore down the stage and talked with the students it would be 11:00 before we walked out of the auditorium. Here we were in a town we knew nothing about. Where do we go to eat? We decided to drive down the main drag and around campus trying to find a place that was appealing, always relying on the spirits to guide us.

We find a familiar sign... the good old Outback steakhouse. We were seated, feeling like old toads. There were so many young men and women. It has become habit for the both of us to hand out our business cards when having a conversation with an unknown individual. We were tired and hungry; thinking to ourselves that warm bread and butter was going to hit the spot.

As soon as we are settled into our seats this cute little waitress came walking up to our table. Her bright white teeth shining in the lights. We ordered our drinks. We have finally learned not to order an appetizer... they bring more than enough food. Like clockwork, Brad pulled out one of our business cards, laying it on the table where it could be easily seen. After learning of our mission and our tragedy, we always receive better service, and we never know, the spirits have led us to people that have helped us open many doors.

I'll name this waitress Terry. Terry set our drinks on the table her eyes focusing on our card. She read it out loud: *GHB KILLS*. Her reaction was "Oh my God, what is this about?" We began telling her of Michael, tears began to well up in her eyes, and her mouth opened wide in shock and dismay.

Wiping tears away, Terry began sharing her own experience with GHB. Terry was at one of the local bars; she had been there before. She had gone that evening with friends. Sometime during the evening, one of her so-called friends slipped GHB into her drink. Within fifteen minutes she began to feel different. Her vision became blurry, her speech was slurred, and she told us of her body becoming numb. She said it felt like when your arms and legs go to sleep.

Terry fell out of the chair, landing on the floor. The owner of the bar must have seen this before, because he called 911. This is Terry's description of her fight to stay alive and not die.

Terry explained that when she arrived at the hospital she began to wake up. The first thing she noticed was her breathing. Her body was starving for oxygen. Terry was gasping for air. She remembered the doctor shining his light into her eyes and hearing the doctor call to her. *Terry, can you hear me? This is the doctor.* The doctor asked her to squeeze his hand, asking her *can you feel this?* The doctor kept asking Terry "what did you take, what are you on?" Terry's breathing continued to slow down to where she labored to breath. The doctor had to put her on a respirator. She could hear the doctor and nurses calling out to her, hoping she would respond. Terry shared that she tried desperately to move her fingers, arms, legs, and toes. She said she couldn't even move her eyes. Terry had never been so scared before in her life.

While Terry shared her experience with us, this put us back into Michael's room that Friday morning. Our hearts literally pounded. We squirmed in our seats, wiping tears away. Brad will never forget Michael's eyes, the terror that he saw in his eyes and face. This still haunts Brad today. Terry said, "I'm sorry for telling you this, but I just had to." The three of us were wiping tears. We stood up and gave her a hug.

We didn't eat much of our dinner. Our hunger was gone. We had knots in our stomach. How could we possibly eat? We both had gigantic lumps in our throats. Seeing Michael in our mind trying desperately to roll over, wanting to call out for his mother. Our minds replayed that night, asking his friends many, many times if Michael was on anything. Being told, "No, honest, we just smoked pot." Brad remembered standing at the edge of our bed next to where Debbie was laying. He debated that night, thinking should he ask Debbie to get a chair and go sit in Michael's room to make sure he would be all right through the night. Debbie was still going through the process of healing from cervical spine surgery. Brad kept thinking; Michael's friends reassured him that he had just smoked pot.

Less than two hours later, Brad was standing before college students reliving Michael's last day of his life sharing the wrong choices he and his friends made that fateful day. Now, truly understanding what our son experienced while he lay there, knowing that he was dying. Replaying this in our mind as Brad told his story brought tears to his eyes, a lump in his throat and knots in his gut that caused him to stop speaking many times. He would press hard to recapture his composure to carry on and continue to share our emotional story.

Chapter Twelve

Her Twin Sister

Debbie had scheduled some high schools in the northeastern part of the state by Jacksonville. On many occasions, we are blessed by a local newspaper publishing an article about our mission, "Michael's Message." The Jacksonville paper published an article that was very informative and terrific. A mother came home from work and while reading her evening newspaper found the headline of a mother and father losing their son to the date rape drug GHB This mother could relate to our story—her daughter had a blind date with this drug. The mother read the article, and she just couldn't get it out of her mind. The newspaper company made sure people would be able to contact us; our e-mail, phone number, and business address were published.

We arrived home after being gone all week. One of Debbie's enjoyments is reading our e-mails. Many times there are letters from students that we had just visited the past week. The letters range from raw to poignant to grateful to sad, but they are always heartfelt. This time she received a letter from a mother. Just a short note stating her daughter had been given GHB, could we meet? Debbie made contact with this mother. We were scheduled to be back in her area the following month, and arrangements were made to have dinner with them. I will name the two girls Marcia and Loretta.

Loretta began to explain New Year's night. She went to a party with friends. A college student slipped GHB, also known as the date rape drug, into her drink. No one seemed to know who this young man was. Loretta doesn't remember, or never knew how she arrived home. She has no idea what time she arrived. Loretta was left at home on her own sometime in the night. Her twin sister went to work New Year's Day. That morning her intuition, her inner voice, began to send her information that her sister was in danger and needed help.

This inner voice kept prodding her until she left work. She drove directly to Loretta's home, where she lived with her mother and brother. Her sister arrived finding her twin unconscious, face down on the floor. Loretta looked purple, had no pulse, and would not respond. Paramedics were called to the scene, and she was rushed to the hospital. The emergency room doctor took her vitals; Loretta was taking in one breath per minute and she was pronounced braindead. The emergency room doctor advised her twin to call family members and the family clergymen because he did not expect Loretta to live.

Her family and friends were baffled. Loretta never acquainted herself with drugs, but the doctor told them she was dying from a drug overdose. What the drug was, the doctor had no idea. Her family raced to find the people she was with and what took place the night before. The information would be vital if Loretta was to have a chance to live. Loretta's friends thought they were doing the right thing making sure she got home safe. Home safe???? There is no safe where GHB is concerned. Loretta was already in what is called a G-hole by the time her friends got her home. They thought, she would "sleep it off". But it is impossible to sleep off an overdose of GHB.

Loretta's mother was notified. She happened to be seven hours from home somewhere in South Carolina celebrating the New Year. Her mother's trip back home was the longest trip home she had ever made, even though she and her son were traveling 90 miles per hour sometimes over 100. We were told the trip only took them five hours. Her mother told us she prayed every mile home.

Her mother walked into the emergency room to find her daughter lifeless with a machine breathing for her, tubes sticking in every cavity of her body. The doctor told her Loretta wouldn't make it and that she was brain-dead. This is a mother's worst nightmare only this was no dream. Her family was forced to weather the storm, because of an inconsiderate human being. Loretta's mother stood by her bedside, her heart pounding wildly praying to GOD for help. She begged to have the privilege of having Loretta continue to be in her life and to not be taken away from her. Even if it meant caring for Loretta for a lifetime, she would accept that dilemma just as long as she could keep her. This family was so very lucky; Loretta came out of her coma 12 hours later.

Doctors and medical staff could not believe her recovery. Loretta was back to being herself with only a few minimal residual defects. Loretta has problems with her eyesight; she has an exasperating situation with her short-term memory. She will often lose her thought in the middle of a conversation. She can no longer remember names. With this problem, Loretta has an extremely difficult problem with learning. Reading a newspaper or a book is challenging because she cannot remember what she just read, so it is impossible for her to learn. This came from someone slipping this liquid that looks like water into her drink. Loretta continues with her recovery from her blind date.

Chapter Thirteen

Graduation 2001

May was a tough month for Deb and me. As well as all of Michael's family and loved ones. Debbie received an email from one of Michael's classmates. The female student stated she had known Michael for a long time. She wrote of how they would meet at school on the patio and talk until the bell rang for class. She told Debbie that they (Michael's friends) have not forgotten a truly wonderful human being, and when they walked across the stage in June there would be one courageous individual who would be missing. Some of Michael's classmates asked to remember Michael at their graduation, but their principal and teachers would not allow any statements about our son. I do agree with their decision. That special day should be about achievements and happy memories.

We were heartbroken, though. Michael's school scheduled graduation on our son's *18th birthday, June 1st*.

We should have been able to have a joyous weekend taking pictures, having a family gathering, Uncle Brad making his famous milkshakes. None of this transpired because of wrong choices by Michael and his friends. I believe because of Michael's death, it was too hard for his close friends to comprehend. Some didn't graduate; they also missed prom and other school activities, they chose a road of self-destruction.

Debbie walked around this house, tears flooding her eyes continuously. The cemetery is still one of our regular stops. So on his birthday his mother bought balloons; one read congratulations on graduation, another said happy birthday, and thinking of you. Debbie came out of the store with these big balloons I expected her to float up to the sky at anytime.

We drove up to Michael's grave and realized some of his classmates had dropped by. We found white roses, cards, and a little stuffed panther, the school mascot. Also resting on the grave was a graduation cap from which a tassel dangled saying class of 2001. This melted our hearts, brought us to tears, with feelings of pride and sadness we were very humbled. Michael's classmates even with their busy schedules getting prepared for graduation took the time to drop by his grave and express Michael you're not forgotten. Thank you class of 2001.

However, our greatest wish would be that never again would teens in America have to visit a gravesite for a classmate killed because of drugs. Imagine if drug abuse didn't exist. If there were no tragic DUI crashes. No overdoses. All teens deserve to grow up and grow old, to graduate, find love, go to college, get a job, get married, start a family.

So we ask you, every reader, to help our dream come true.

Father's Day: The Yearbook

After graduation, the next celebrated event was Father's Day. We no longer celebrate the two days dedicated for parents. This Father's Day I was granted a wonderful surprise. Michael's high school dedicated a memorial page for our son in the yearbook. The yearbook committee did an awesome job. They were so kind to us, they treated me special, this year on Father's Day. His senior class presented the yearbook to me on this special day. Michael had some special wonderful friends in his class. I thank you again Westwood High class of 2001. The yearbook has a place in our hearts we share it with many and plan on taking it on the road with us when we are working our drug awareness program. We will continue to share our struggle learning to live without our Michael; again in hopes it will help prevent another family from enduring the tragedy and the enormous loss we must learn to live with.

Michael: Who Would You Leave Behind?

Chapter Fourteen

Our Schools

As I sit down to write the last pages of this book, I took the time to read many letters that Michael's mother and I have received on our journeys traveling to many schools sharing our Drug Awareness Program, Michael's Message.

While reading these letters I had a tissue in my hand wiping my tears away. The information that many students share of the drug war that is handed to them on a daily basis is frightening. While reading these letters describing the difficulties of just getting through the day, trying desperately to stay focused, I realized the love and sincerity these student's shared.

Students today have to put on their coat of armor as soon as they climb on the school bus or step out of their mother or fathers car walking to the entrance of their school. We are all taught to keep good friends and to stay away from negative environments, yet we plunge our children into an environment where they have to say no every day.

Our places of work have a more positive environment than our children's schools. Here's a quote from a seventeen-year-old junior high school student. *"The prevalence of drugs scares me!"* Or this one: *"You can't go into the bathroom without choking on the air from smoke or walk through the halls without hearing people bragging about the high they got from painkillers, or any drug for that matter."*

Some of our teens are persuaded to believe illegal drug use is so popular it has become their favorite pastime. Another quote: *"It is almost impossible to walk down the halls Monday morning without hearing someone talking about how they got wasted or baked over the weekend!"*

Another quote *"Our generation is, in fact, plagued with massive drug use."* I have had many students tell me there is so much drug activity in their schools that you can have the choice of the drug you want.

I know young people who chose to drop out of school, not because they couldn't make the grade, but because they knew if they continued the peer pressure would have made them so uncomfortable they would become an addict if they continued school. These young loving people work in the foodservice industry, and most of them achieved their GEDs. They told me they are better off having dropped out than to have drugs take over their lives or ending up in the judicial system. Some of these young people have, after earning their GEDs, continued their college education.

How insane is this? Our schools are drug supermarkets not institutions of learning. How has it come to this?

I thought a lot about this quote *"Most people don't know what it is like to have to say no every day!"* With that statement, I don't blame our teachers or members of the faculty in our schools. The teachers and principals that Debbie and I have had the honor to meet are devoted, great, and loving human beings with enormous hearts. These great people have a special love for their kids, their students. We saw dedicated people, amazing people who want to create a better world by being teachers.

The new schools that are being built are of enormous size. Students lose their identity because of the population. These schools being built sit on 40 acres of land and the student population is 2,000 and above. Can the principal know every child by name? The teachers haven't the time to have a one-on-one rapport with each student. There are more students in one of these schools than the population of the town that I grew up in.

In the sports program, stop and think of how many students are cut or turned down from being able to be a player on the team. In the student body, there is one president, and only a few positions available. How many students lose the privilege and honor of achieving that goal.

We say that keeping busy keeps our kids off drugs, yet programs are cut at schools because of budgets. No sports. No arts. When are our kids, our future, going to be the number one priority?

Heroin In The Boy's Bathroom

I cannot forget Michael coming home from school, this was the beginning of the school year, his last year of school. Just two months before he died. The day he walked in the boy's bathroom and witnessed a classmate-injecting heroin into his arm. I'll never forget that evening. Michael's face was so expressive. He seemed so sad, his feelings hurt. He was depressed about the whole incident. His mother sensed that something was troubling him. She tried to console him, asking him what was wrong. Michael went to his room and shut the door. He was in there for two hours. His mother was in the laundry room taking clothes out of the washer getting them ready for the dryer. Michael came out of his room searching for his mother. I heard him say "Mommy." I knew it was serious when I heard him say *mommy*. I followed him to the laundry room. I was standing behind him, but he was unaware of me standing there. I will never forget what Michael said, "Mommy, I saw a boy shoot up heroin in the boys' bathroom today!" His mother almost jumped into the washer.

I remember seeing this done just one time and then I thought it was one of the most disgusting acts a human could do to their own body. It was sickening! I was a grown man, in my twenties, and I got as far away from that situation as I could immediately. I can imagine my little boy seeing this, and being at school of all places.

He didn't have a choice, that choice of getting away from that environment. We, his mother and Dad, made him go there five days a week, eight hours a day. We were trying to be protective to be good parents. We went to his school the very next day making the principal aware of this sick behavior. Michael was called out of class. He was mortified that we were there. When asked for the boy's name, Michael said he didn't know the boy or he wouldn't tell. When I drove him home from the meeting, I felt like his principal and the other staff emphasized to Michael, "you don't tell everything you see." Sure enough when we got home from school that evening he told me he wished he hadn't told us, he could get jumped, even killed for opening his mouth.

I remember him telling me in one of our discussions, that he had to say "NO" to someone offering him drugs every day at school. Since the birth of Michael's Message, Inc., A Drug Awareness Program, we have spent hours with students. The information we get from students, sixth grade through high school and on into college, is that my son **was not** exaggerating all.

Michael: Who Would You Leave Behind?

Chapter Fifteen

Looking Back on Michael's Last Day

Michael's last day was like any other normal school day. When he woke up and looked in the mirror, did the thought flash through his mind, *I'll have to say no to drugs sometime today.* He walked out that door like he had done so many mornings with his friends at his side walking a fast pace to catch the bus. My guess is he didn't have that thought exactly—because drugs were so much a part of the teen culture that it had become a simple fact of life.

His friends told us, that while walking to his third-hour class, he was complaining to his friend that he had a headache. Another student overheard the conversation and offered Michael pills to get rid of his headache. Michael, assuming the pills were some kind of aspirin, made the choice to take them.

We were told he took these pills throughout the day. When he came home from school that evening his body was telling him he was overloading it, contaminating it, his temple, his body. His mother and I had no clue he had been taking any kind of pill.

With his mind cloudy from the methadone, which he assumed to be aspirin, another choice came confronting him. His friend brought GHB to Michael's bedroom. We do not know why Michael took GHB; we only know that it was a wrong and deadly choice. This normal day turned out to be Michael's and his community's worst day. There were so very many saddened hearts. I'll never forget the day of his funeral. After the service at the cemetery, his loved ones began to walk to their cars, the sun shining bright, no clouds and then, just a few rain drops. I will always believe these drops were tears from heaven, just enough to make you take notice but not to really get anyone wet.

Knowing Michael Was a Privilege

Michael was only 15 years old when his life here on earth was stolen from all of us. He was a loving, kindhearted person who was wise beyond his years. Michael liked to be with people that laughed, and he enjoyed life. I believe he accepted people for who they were. Michael was a classmate that you might not have seen every day, but you were aware of his presence.

Through Michael's years in school he achieved citizen of the month, even citizen of the year demonstrating his love by helping a classmate put on her shoes at the bowling alley and carrying her ball. She had injured her arm and was unable to tie her shoes. He had so very much love and joy that he did share while he was here with us. I miss his hugs. He would walk up to me and put his arms around me giving me a kiss on the forehead. There were times his friends would see this. I could see in their faces that they didn't receive this at their homes, the confused look, and the envied expressions that appeared on their young faces.

In elementary school Michael worked to be a guard at the crosswalks to make sure everyone was safe. He took a lot of pride putting on his bright orange strap. I feel that he felt just as important as his uncle, who was stationed across the street at the firehouse. His uncle was one of his heroes. At this time in his life he was strictly against drugs and if he saw any activity of this kind such as smoking tobacco he would report this negative activity.

In fifth grade he was very active in the DARE program. The school resource officer and the DARE program instructor were two more of his heroes. Michael had a great interest in the DARE program. He was strictly against any kind of drug activity.

After fifth grade there were no more classes to reinforce his strength to continue to stay focused and say "NO" when he was asked to take something and to report the incident. Michael did have these circumstances in his life, and he did say no and he did report the activity. I look back at these situations and when he did the right thing there were no rewards. The reward he received was by some older peer threatening him, telling him to keep his mouth shut, and being ridiculed by more of his peers. The older he got, the more of this he saw. And as time went on he saw more and more friends being persuaded into this activity. The message that he received getting older, maturing, was to be like the rest of them, to have their approval and to be liked by his friends.

Michael: Who Would You Leave Behind?

Chapter Sixteen

The Ending

The day Deb and I buried our son, I stood near his grave. I watched as they lowered him into his vault. I walked around his grave after they sealed it. I wanted to be sure his lid was on correct and sealed tight. I stood back and watched them cover my son with dirt. The job was finished, but I found myself not wanting to leave.

Finally, my brother-in-law gently tugged on my sleeve and said it was time to go. As I turned my back and we started down the hill, I thought this was my last assignment as Michael's father.

When Michael came to me in the dream, and he asked his mother and I to tell his friends and his generation of his tragic story, well, we as all good parents try to give or do what our children ask of us, his mother and I are doing as he asked. As we travel sharing Michael's Message, we ask for your prayers, support and love. When you see us in our travels, please come up to us and give us a hug, and may GOD be with you and yours. On our journey we are striving to save another family from having to live this loss and endure the enormous pain and suffering we live with. Our goal is to serve others so this world we live in will be better and safer.

Michael was a dreamer and a doer, a minority of his generation. His mother and I will take his dream to educate and bring love to all. So as I say goodbye, and you close this book, please take this great opportunity and privilege to hug and kiss your children. Take time to hear their stories for they will have their own, just don't expect them to give names, their lives will be in danger. Get involved. Let's make a difference.

I often think of Michael's last night, and I'm so thankful his mother and I received a kiss from him before putting him to bed. Our last words were "I love you." I have people tell me that, "I didn't get to tell them, or I wish I would have told them." Please make it a house rule that you kiss, hug, and express your love when walking out the door or getting that goodnight kiss.

And please remember, a simple mistake, an error in judgment, can cost you your life. Taking a drink or soda from someone you don't know well, not using the buddy system at parties to make sure you both stay safe, or trying drugs. One mistake could be your last.

And who would you leave behind?